Under The Lim

recipes by Nikki Emmerton
photography by Sean Dylan Williams

more
soulful
homemade
vegan &
veggie
recipes from

Under The
Lime Tree

spa b & b
france

Pyjama Press www.pyjamapress.com

First published in the UK 2017 by Pyjama Press.

A CIP catalogue record for this book is available from the British Library.

Design by Pyjama Press, UK.

Layout by Nikki Emmerton.

Photography by Sean Dylan Williams.

Printed and bound in the UK or USA by Lightning Source Ltd.

ISBN: 978-1-908000-34-7

About us

Although it's hard to believe now, we haven't always been running UTLT. Born in Trinidad, my previous incarnation in business led to an illness, a world trip, a chance massage, a new career and to running a Spa B&B in the french countryside. Born in Johannesburg, Sean's previous incarnation led him to Australia, a career in marine science, a homecoming and a chance meeting with me in a local bar in the french countryside. Many moons have waxed and waned since 2004, but together we've developed UTLT into The Place to B & Be. Collaborating with Sean on this second recipe book has been great fun. We've combined our skills and shared our passions and created a little book of the updated repertoire of recipes at Under The Lime Tree. These recipes have grown organically as demand for vegan or gluten-free or dairy-free or raw food increases, and they've grown out of our own desire to be mindful of what we eat without compromising on fun, simplicity or flavour. Like the first book, they're an example of our daily diet and demonstrate how easy it is to make uncomplicated meals that look good and taste good and are good for you. In fact, it constantly amazes me how much natural goodness there is in the most ordinary of fruits, the most humble of vegetables, in the smallest of seeds, how much they all deserve 'super-food' status and how little we need to do to harness all that goodness, naturally. I hope they inspire you to make more of vegetables, to include nuts and seeds, to love legumes, to play with colours, textures and flavours, to use your imagination to tweak them in ways that suit you best and to be mindful of your meals what ever you eat. All of the ingredients in this book are widely available. All except for Sean that is! A major ingredient in life at Under The Lime Tree, he's not to be consumed off the premises. I'll also check your bags to make sure you haven't stashed Nellie or Toby either.

Nikki . ♡

"Thank you" from Us at UTLT

Wonderful things have been said about us, about our home and about the life we lead at UTLT. It's very rewarding to feel so inspired by our guests and humbling to think that we might inspire others in return. The participation of everyone who's been here and the anticipation of everyone still to come motivates and stimulates us to keep doing what we love do. Our collaboration on this book is a validation of our team work, and a celebration that good food, good conversation and good company are still the simple pleasures in life to be adored and cherished.

Merci à tous, à bientôt et très bon appétit

"A perfect place to relax, thanks Nikki and Sean for everything." Sue

"Paradise comes to mind. Thank you for sharing it with us. You both make it seem so effortless! Fantastic food and good company." Glynn and Pearl

"What wonderful hosts. Wonderful food, consistently delicious, creative and colourful." Sarah and Rikki

"Nikki et Sean sont des hôtes incomparables, toujours disponibles et à l'écoute dans un superbe cadre campagnard; parfait!" Maxime

"Quel magnifique week-end nous avons passé en votre compagnie! Merci pour toutes les choses que nous avons partagé, nouriture incroyable, sérénité, belles étoiles. A très vites!" Fabian et Elodie

"We have been here only one week but it feels like a whole month thanks to the two of you! Wonderful! Your place is great to stay at, with lovely conversations and such tasteful food. Cheers to new friendships!" Jerome and Nicole

"Together you and Sean complete this intoxicating place, nurturing and nourishing your guests, or as I feel now, a friend." Joanne

Recipes

Don't be nervous
if you have never
cooked globe
artichokes before

Lots of people don't know what to do with fresh artichoke globes but when in season, they're one of the simplest and easiest vegetables to add to your diet, and in terms of their benefits, they're great for assisting digestion and liver function.

The heart of the globe is the fleshiest and tastiest part, but each outside leaf also has some flesh on it, getting fleshier towards the centre. Drag the flesh off between your teeth then discard the rest of the leaf ~ very primitive and good fun.

great to eat

Globe Artichoke
with a piquant chilli & garlic dressing

1 Three quarter fill a large sauce pan with water. Cut the globes in half, lengthways, and baste with the lemon juice to stop them discolouring. Plunge immediately into the boiling water (they should be completely covered). Boil vigorously for 15 minutes.

2 Meanwhile, make the dressing. Heat the sesame oil in a small frying pan and toss in the garlic and chilli. Fry together for a minute or two. Set aside.

3 When the globes are ready, drain very well by turning them upside down into a colander. Place cut side up in a baking tray and using a tea spoon, scoop out the furry hairs at the base of the heart.

4 Pop under a hot grill for 2 minutes.

5 Take out, spoon the garlic and chilli dressing over the heads, crack sea salt and black pepper over, and pop back under the grill for another minute.

Serve immediately. Good as an appetiser or a starter

1 globe or head per person
juice of 1 lemon per globe
a large pan of boiling water
3 table spoons sesame oil
3 garlic cloves, crushed
1 red chilli, finely chopped
sea salt & black peppercorns to season

Other dressings will work equally well. Just make sure they are nice and piquant to pick out the flavour of the artichoke.

In summer our garden is resplendent ...

... with globe artichokes reaching out in all directions to dominate and choke the skyline. They're wonderful to watch ~ the heads blooming and opening continuously until, all of a sudden, they've burst into full flower and you've lost the chance to harvest them! No matter, they become the most marvellous flowers and continue to bewitch us from the kitchen window and provide food for insects & wildlife for weeks to come.

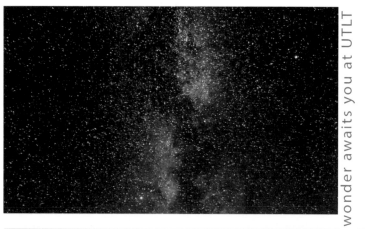

Did you know

~ red, orange and yellow spells good?

Pumpkins are power-packed with iron, vitamins C and E and other antioxidants, most particularly, carotenes which give the flesh it's red or yellow colour.

All red, orange or yellow fleshed veg ~ sweet potatoes, carrots, other squashes ~ are strongly linked to a lower risk of heart disease, stroke, some cancers and cataracts.

Go red
with your veg

Tangy Thai Pumpkin Soup

Ridiculously easy, velvety smooth, delightfully delicious

This tangy soup is a great way to warm up on winter evenings. When the sky is clear, I love to gaze at the stars with our large reflector telescope. We cradle our bowls of hot soup afterwards, amazed at what we've seen

1 Split the pumpkin in half and then into wedges. Remove the seeds from each wedge, season and dry roast to deepen its natural nutty flavour. This also helps to loosen the skin. Measure out 750g of flesh.

2 In a large pan, gently sauté the onion, chilli and ginger in the oil until the onion is transparent. Add the roasted pumpkin, then turn off the heat.

3 Stir in the coconut milk and leave to cool.

4 When cooled, add the zest and lime juice and a handful of coriander.

5 Blend in batches until velvety smooth and return to the pan.

6 Gently heat through, drizzling in as much vegetable stock as desired to get a thick creamy consistency.

7 Check seasoning. Ladle into mugs or bowls, squeeze a lime wedge over, garnish with a sprinkle of desiccated coconut and chopped coriander.

Serve hot and look up at the stars

750g roasted pumpkin

1 red onion, chopped

1 inch fresh ginger, grated

1 red chilli (or more for a hotter taste!), chopped

1 table spoon vegetable oil

400ml coconut milk

400ml vegetable stock

zest & juice of 1 lime plus 2 more for garnish, quartered

2 generous handfuls of fresh coriander

2 table spoons desiccated coconut

9

Simple and versatile

fun finger food

Spring rolls can be so versatile: use strips of cucumber, carrot, avocado, cooked tofu, red, orange and yellow peppers ... or roll into sheets of filo and bake for a warm winter wrap.

This recipe makes about 8 rolls, although the final number depends on how you roll 'em. Rice paper can be a bit tricky to use, and can tear easily, but it's also more robust than you realise.

dipping delights

Fresh Spring Rolls

These delicately delicious rolls are fun finger-food to snack on or to present as a starter to a stir-fry main dish

1 Gently heat the sesame oil, chilli, ginger, lemon juice and sugar in a large pan. Add the cabbages first, if using, and stir-fry quickly for a minute or so. Add the other shredded and grated veg (except for the whole leaves) and continue stirring for a couple of minutes until well mixed together. Set aside.

2 Quarter fill a large flan dish with warm water. The temperature of the water must be comfortable enough to dip your fingers into. The dish must be bigger than the rice sheets. Prepare a flat rolling space and place a damp tea towel on it. Have ready a serving plate to put the rolls onto.

3 Gently take one rice sheet and place it in the warmed water. Keep hold of it and when it softens, carefully lift it out and place it flat onto the tea towel.

4 Place a whole spinach or lettuce leaf near the edge of the rice paper nearest to you. Put a couple of dessert spoons of filling onto the middle of the leaf, packing it gently into a fat cigar shape with your fingers. Leave a gap either side of the leaf so that the sides can be folded in.

5 Hold the filling in place while picking up the front edge of the rice sheet and roll away from you, tucking the mixture in and folding in the edges as you go. Place onto the serving plate and roll another.

Try to have the same amount of filling in each roll. Make as many rolls as either the rice sheets or your filling allows. You might need to add more water to the flan dish to keep it warm. Can be made in advance and kept refrigerated until ready to serve

makes 8

1 packet rice paper (about 10 round sheets)

100g shredded leafy greens such as spinach, lettuce, kale, as well as red or green cabbage. Keep aside a whole spinach or lettuce leaf per roll

100g carrot, grated

100g courgette, grated

3 spring onions, sliced lengthways

2 table spoons sesame oil

1 red chilli, finely chopped

fresh ginger, thumb size, grated

juice of 1 lemon

1 tea spoon brown sugar

a side serving per person of soy sauce, sweet & sour sauce, pickled ginger, and if you dare, wasabi for dipping

11

Roasted Red Pepper Dip

A super simple snack to make your mouth water

1 Drain the red peppers well by placing between paper towels and patting dry.

2 Place in a food processor and blitz with the red onion, chilli pepper, lime juice and parsley leaves for 2 seconds.

3 Add your other ingredients, whether vegan or veggie, and blitz again briefly. Salt to taste.

Serve topped with more red pepper, more parsley, black olives, toasted pine nuts, or roll into chargrilled courgette wraps, or serve with crudities & crisps and scoop up with toasted tortillas ...

the basics

250g roasted red peppers from a jar, drained & chopped

1 red onion, chopped

1 red chilli pepper, chopped

¼ lime, juiced

handful parsley leaves, reserving some for garnish

salt

vegan version

1 jar chickpeas, drained

2 garlic cloves, chopped

veggie version

250g ricotta or other soft cheese

80g roquefort, crumbled

delish with ...

preprandial dinner drinks

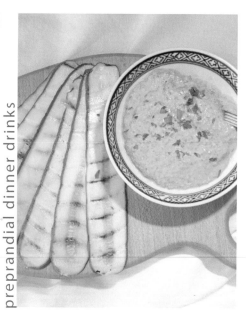

Melon Salsa Boats

When in season, fresh melons add an exotic flourish to jazz up everyday ingredients like cherry tomatoes, red onions, olives, artichoke or avocado. Add a sprinkle of ginger, a dash of chilli pepper, a crack of sea salt, some toasted pine nuts, and a final flourish of nigella seeds et voilà ~ a simple, unusual and tasty snack to feast on

1 Cut a whole melon into quarters and remove the seeds. Without cutting the skin, score the flesh of each segment in half lengthways then criss-cross horizontally, or scoop the flesh into a bowl and reserve the skin boats for serving.

2 Sprinkle over the ginger and chilli powders, add a crack of sea salt and simply add some of your favourite toppings.

3 My favourites are ... avocado, artichoke, cherry tomatoes, sun-dried tomatoes, olives, fresh mango, roasted red pepper, red onion, toasted pine nuts, usually something leafy green like rocket or watercress and always nigella seeds.

You really can add a little of what you like ~ simple

the basics

¹melon
¹tea spoon ginger powder
½ tea spoon chilli powder
sea salt & nigella seeds

topping choices

avocado· artichoke· cherry tomatoes· sun·dried tomatoes· olives· fresh mango· roasted red pepper· red onion· toasted pine nuts· something leafy green like rocket or watercress· plus nigella seeds

Did you know

Nigella sativa: the remedy for everything except death

Nigella Seed is also known as black seed, black cumin, black caraway, black onion, Roman coriander. Whilst it's common name might be in dispute, the health benefits of this tiny but terrific little wonder are in no doubt – they've even been referred to as the remedy for "everything but death". They have anti-inflammatory, anti-bacterial, anti-fungal, anti-convulsive, anti-asthmatic effects. They've been known to reduce cancerous cells, reduce blood pressure, lower blood sugar levels and boost overall heart health. What's not to like? Sprinkle them over anything and everything.

easy peasy Fig Chutney

for you to serve it with

½ cup brown sugar

½ cup apple cider vinegar

² cups figs

½ cup apples, diced

½ cup red onion, chopped

½ cup raisins

¹ stick cinnamon

½ tea spoon ground ginger

½ tea spoon ground cardamom

½ tea spoon salt)

1 Soak the raisins in a bowl of water for 10 minutes.

2 Melt the sugar with the vinegar in a large saucepan. Add all other ingredients, and the raisins when they are ready.

3 Bring to the boil for a minute then reduce to a simmer and cook gently for an hour, stirring frequently. Pour into sterilised jars and store.

Eat with
relish old bean

Chick Pea Loaf

Chick peas have long been the 'bean du jour' but now it's cooking liquid, aquafaba, is sweeping across vegan kitchens as the new egg-white replacement. Don't dump it down the drain again

1 Heat the oven to 200C / gas 6.

2 Grease and line a loaf tin.

3 Sift the flour, bicarbonate of soda, baking powder and spices together into a large bowl.

4 Add the chopped onion, frozen peas, sun-dried tomatoes, chickpeas, olive oil and pinch of salt. Add the water and mix all ingredients together well. It will be very thick.

5 For the vegan version, add a pinch of salt to the reserved chickpea water or aquafaba, and whisk for 2 minutes. Gently fold the mixture into the mix and pour into the lined tin.

6 For the veggie version, add 1 beaten egg and fold into the mix. Pour into the lined tin.

7 Bake for approximately 1 hour.

Test with a knife that the centre is cooked – it should come out clean

Gluten free, wheat free, dairy free and nutritious to nibble on with chutneys or cheeses

220g chick pea flour
1 tea spoon bicarbonate of soda
1 tea spoon baking powder
1 tea spoon ginger
1 tea spoon turmeric (curcuma)
½ tea spoon chilli powder
1 red onion, chopped
120g frozen peas
7 sun-dried tomatoes, chopped
100g chickpeas (reserve the water)
100ml olive oil
pinch of salt
130ml water

vegan version
50ml chickpea water (aquafaba)
pinch of salt

veggie version
1 egg

15

Cabbage ~ an unsung superhero

Available in many varieties, the seemingly mundane cabbage is high in fibre and contains so many nutritional superpowers that it is a must-have magical veg to include regularly in your diet.

And red is best when it comes to the wide variety available. It's higher in antioxidants which can reduce inflammation, provide cancer protection and boost brain function.

for the salad

¼ red cabbage, shredded

5 sun-dried tomatoes, sliced

2 table spoons mango or other spiced chutney

1 beetroot, cooked

bunch of rocket

salt & pepper

topping

any number of foods with contrasting colours · here fresh marigold leaves, but slices of mango, cherry tomatoes, radish, red onion or seeds of any kind would also be great

Traffic light salads ~ RED
red cabbage, beetroot & sun dried tomatoes

1 Blanche the red cabbage in boiling water for a minute, drain and set aside to cool. (The cooking water will turn blue, so I don't usually use it again).

2 In a large bowl mix it in with the mango (or other) chutney and sliced sun-dried tomatoes.

3 Prepare a serving dish with the rocket leaves.

4 Arrange a circle of sliced beetroot around the edge and pile the red cabbage/mango mix in the middle.

5 Crack salt & black pepper over and top with whatever takes your fancy.

Traffic light salads ~ AMBER
celeriac & carrot with sunflower seeds

Not the most appetising vegetable to look at, celeriac is from the same botanical family as celery and although it has similar overtones, it is much more earthy, intense and nutty in flavour

Celeriac

Cut all that knobbly skin off with a knife until you're left with a creamy yellow flesh that can be cooked or eaten raw. Low in calories but high in vitamins and minerals it's a great addition to, or substitute for, potato dishes.

¼ of a celeriac· grated

½ lemon· juiced

²carrots· grated

dressing

¹ table spoon of Dijon mustard

² table spoons of walnut oil or sesame oil

¹ dessert spoon raspberry vinegar

salt & pepper to taste

topping

a pinch of nigella seeds

a handful of sunflower seeds

chopped parsley

1 Grate the celeriac into a bowl and immediately squeeze over the lemon juice to stop it discolouring.

2 Add the grated carrot.

3 Whisk all the dressing ingredients together with a fork, mix through the celeriac and carrot.

4 Then top with nigella seeds, sunflower seeds and the chopped parsley or other toppings of your choice.

17

Cabbage

The unglamorous green cabbage
is a garden favourite available
throughout the year.

Blanching briefly or steaming for
a second simply takes the super-
crunch out of it, but take care not
to overcook and loose all those
lovely health benefits.

Traffic light salads ~ GREEN
cabbage & cucumber with goji berries

A so-simple
~ super-food salad that's sumptuous to look at and sensational to serve up

¼ spring green cabbage, shredded

100g mangetout (flat peas)

1 tea spoon vegetable stock

¼ cucumber, chopped

¼ red onion, finely sliced

bunch of rocket

dressing
2 garlic cloves, minced

3 table spoons good olive oil

1 table spoon lemon juice

salt & pepper

topping
handful goji berries

handful dried cranberries

1 Discard one or two outer layers of the cabbage and shred about a quarter of it. (The rest will keep well wrapped in the fridge ready for another recipe).

2 Pop it into a pan of boiling water along with the vegetable stock and mangetout, then blanche for a minute. Scoop all the veg out with a slotted spoon into a colander to drain, then set aside on a tea towel to cool. (Reserve the cooking water for another dish).

3 Meanwhile, wash and chop the cucumber and prepare the onion.

4 When cooled, mix the cucumber and onion in with the cabbage and mangetout.

5 Place all the dressing ingredients in a jar and shake thoroughly then pour over the cabbage salad and fold in.

Top with the goji and cranberries sprinkled over

Goji berries ~ the Tonic of Tibet

These shrivelled little bright red berries are treated with such respect in Tibet, there are celebrations held in honour of them! Known to strengthen the immune system, they are abundantly packed with vitamins, nutrients, anti-oxidants, complex compounds and minerals which makes them a marvellous addition to any diet. They have a mild tangy taste which is simultaneously sweet and sour. So keep them in your store cupboard and add them to savoury or dessert dishes as a decoration.

Leek and potato
are the perfect pair for a pizza

They are like an old married couple ~ habitually comfortable in each other's company. But you'll need a little something-on-the-side to bring some zing into the companionship and that's where the tapenade comes in. Originating in the Provence region of France, its name comes from the Provençal word for capers, *tapenas*, where the main ingredient was simply capers preserved in olive oil - an authentically peasant paste to add a pungent, salty flavour to any dish.

Tapenade

Nowadays, mostly black olives are puréed or pounded in a pestle and mortar with capers and drizzled with olive oil, but green olive tapenade is also widely available.

Some tapenade versions are flavoured differently with other ingredients such as garlic, herbs, anchovies, lemon juice or even brandy, so do check the ingredients if you're buying from a supermarket.

Avocado
so deserving of the title super food

High in healthy fats, the humble avocado is an abundant source of important minerals, vitamins and nutrients and has more potassium than most plants, even bananas.

The majority of the fat in avocado is oleic acid ~ a monoUNsaturated fatty acid (also the major component in olive oil), believed to be responsible for its beneficial effects.

Fat is essential for every single cell in your body, so don't be fooled by fat-free and low-fat products, or shy away from foods like avocados and nuts that are full of healthy fats.

Pack into parcels if you don't fancy a pizza

Leek & Potato Pizza
with Provençal tapenade & avocado

1 Pre-heat the oven to 220C / gas 7.

2 Remove the outer leaves of the leeks, cut in half lengthways, then into rounds and rinse. Blanche in unsalted boiling water with the vegetable stock. Scoop out with a slotted spoon into a colander, drain and dry thoroughly between kitchen towel.

3 Bring the same cooking water back to the boil and add the potatoes, cooking until soft. Tip out all the water, draining completely. Put the potatoes back in the pan and mash.

4 Scoop out the flesh of the avocado, mash in a bowl and squeeze the slice of lemon over. Add to the mashed potato and mix well. Using the same bowl, mix the leeks with the tea spoon of green olive tapenade. Grate the courgette, pat dry between kitchen towel to get the juices out. Chop the sun dried tomatoes and onions.

5 To build your pizza ~ firstly, have all ingredients ready including cheese, if using. Grease a pizza pan and sprinkle with a little semolina or polenta grains to keep the pastry from sticking and roll in the pastry. Using the back of a spoon, spread the black olive tapenade to the edges, leaving a 2cm gap all around. Add the mashed potato and avocado. Scatter over the grated courgette and pile the leeks on top.

6 Pop in the oven for 20 minutes, then add the sun dried tomatoes, onions and oregano (and cheese if using), before returning to the oven to finish cooking.

2 leeks

500g potatoes, peeled & cubed

1 tea spoon or 1 cube vegetable stock

1 ripe avocado

1 slice of lemon

1 dessert spoon green olive tapenade

½ courgette, grated

4 sun dried tomatoes, finely chopped

½ red onion, finely chopped

1 packet ready-rolled pastry (vegan & GFree pastry are widely available)

1 dessert spoon black olive tapenade

1 tea spoon dried oregano

add an optional topping of your favourite cheese if you fancy

Serve with wine. Oh, did I say that ..?
Well, it's all part of those southern french flavours you're conjuring up in your kitchen, so why not. Santé!

Spirulina
ancient food of the Aztecs

Spirulina was declared one of the best foods for the future in 1974 but it didn't skyrocket in modern popularity until NASA provided it to their astronauts for its superior nutritional profile.

The presence of the pigment phycocyanin is responsible for the rich dark green colouring and it is phycocyanin that gives spirulina it's spiralling superfood status.

Made of up to 70% protein by weight and containing all the amino acids needed for optimal health it contains serious amounts of B vitamins, iron, copper and small amounts of almost every other nutrient we need.

Gram for gram, Spirulina may be the single most nutrient-dense food on earth

No wonder it's worth it's weight in gold

It will cost an arm and a leg, but don't worry about the price – properly stored, it lasts an incredibly long time and in any case, what price good health?

Sprinkle a tiny tea spoonful into soups and curries or onto salads and cereals and add to just about anything you dare to turn green.

You simply can't get cleaner or greener if you include spirulina in your diet

If you do buy some Spiulina, it's absolutely critical to make sure that quality and purity are of the highest standards. Organic is best and Powdered is better since you have to mix it with other food sources to aid digestion and make all that magic available to the body.

Spinach Quiche
with a splash of spirulina

There's no need to use spirulina in this recipe other than it's a supplementary short cut to adding loads of potential nutritional benefits to your diet. Naturally grown around oceans, lakes & ponds, spirulina is a magical micro-organism known as blue-green algae, and it's shockingly healthy

100g dry weight spinach leaves, stalks removed

6 free range organic eggs, separated

1 tea spoon spirulina powder

1 tea spoon turmeric

1 tea spoon salt

1 pot natural greek yogurt

handful of pine nuts

1 packet ready rolled flaky pastry

1 Heat the oven to 200C / gas 6. Grease and line a flan dish.

2 Pick through the spinach and remove any spoiled leaves. Remove the stalks and measure out 100g. Tear up the leaves, place in a colander and rinse with running cold water. Boil a kettle and pour the water over the leaves to wilt them, then drain thoroughly, place between kitchen towel to dry out.

3 Separate the eggs, adding the spirulina and turmeric to the yolks. Beat in the yogurt.

4 Add the spinach leaves and mix well.

5 Whisk the egg whites with the salt for 2 minutes then fold gently into the egg mixture.

6 Roll out the pastry into the flan dish and pour in the egg mix. Sprinkle with the pine nuts and bake for 40 to 50 minutes until the pastry is cooked.

Go even greener

... and serve with a gorgeous green salad and baked sweet potatoes or add some colour to your quiche by adding roasted red pepper slices, black olives, red onion, maybe some roquefort and a spoonful of black olive tapenade.

Lush Variations

~ lasagne, spaghetti, burgers

Take the filling mix and layer it between lasagne sheets, add a creamy garlicky cheesy yummy sauce and voilà, a delicious, nutritious lasagne for later. For a GFree lasagne, substitute the pasta sheets for finely sliced yellow courgette. For spaghetti, simply pile the lentil mixture on top of your favourite noodles or spiralize veg to keep it GFree. For burgers, add breadcrumbs to the mix and shape into patties to fry or roast. Variations are only limited by your imagination.

love lentils ~ giants of the legume family

add them to your diet today

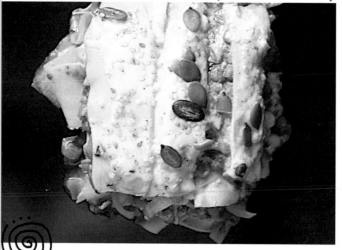

Size doesn't matter ~ when it comes to the small lentil seed, they are nutritionally mighty with virtually no fat & a low calorific content

Lentils are very high in nutritional value, are an excellent source of minerals & vitamins, and are slow burning complex carbohydrates which replenish your iron stores giving you more energy for longer.

Lentils were first cultivated 8,000 years ago. Whole or split they come in a variety of colours, are quick and easy to prepare and are available throughout the year.

A Duo of Lentils
~ for a number of lush dishes

1 Bring to the boil a large saucepan of water. Add the duo of lentils and bring back to the boil before turning down to a simmer until cooked, about 30 to 40 minutes. Add more water if necessary.

2 While the lentils are cooking, put the potatoes on to boil, adding the turmeric and stock to the boiling water. When the potatoes are cooked through, drain and mash with the milk. Season with sea salt to taste. It'll be a lovely golden colour.

3 Pre-heat the oven to 180C / gas mark 4. Heat the oil in a large frying pan on a moderate heat. Add the onions, carrots, courgette and pepper. Stir to mix then add the soy sauce, all the herbs and spices, and tomato sauce. Add the lentils and parsley and mix again.

4 Spoon the filling mix into a baking dish then layer the mashed potato on top, using a fork to spread it evenly. Bake for 30 minutes. Sprinkle over the remaining parsley if using.

Serve hot with a crisp green salad and a nutty bread to scoop up the juices

for the filling

100g green lentils, rinsed in cold water

100g brown lentils, rinsed in cold water

2 table spoons olive oil

1 red onion, chopped

2 carrots, grated

1 courgette, grated

1 yellow bell pepper, chopped

1 dessert spoon dark soy sauce

1 tea spoon powdered black pepper

1 tea spoon dried thyme

1 tea spoon cumin powder

1 tea spoon chilli powder

1 jar good quality tomato sauce

1 handful fresh parsley, with an optional extra for garnish

Shepherd's Pie
~ without the shepherd

A simple take on an old classic ... lovely lentils in a filling that packs a protein-punch.

for the topping

800g potatoes, peeled

1 tea spoon turmeric

1 tea spoon or 1 cube vegetable stock

100g milk (I use soy milk)

25

Moroccan Spiced Sweet Potato Tagine

for the couscous

300ml spiced couscous

50g goji berries

50g dried cranberries

50g pine nuts or slivered almonds

600ml of hot water (re-heat the potato & carrot water)

dash of olive oil

parsley, chopped (or coriander)

1 Pour out the couscous into a measuring jug. Double the measure to get the right quantity of water to add.

2 Put the dry couscous into a wide bottomed serving bowl which you can fit a lid over. Sprinkle the berries and pine nuts (or almonds) on top. Pour over the right amount of boiling water, add the olive oil, cover with the lid and leave to fluff up for 30 minutes.

3 Uncover, fork through when you are ready to serve and sprinkle over the parsley (or coriander).

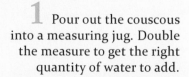

for the dukkha

50g sesame seeds

50g hazelnuts

2 table spoons cumin seeds

2 table spoons coriander seeds

1 tea spoon sea salt

Optional additions
~ 1 table spoon fennel seeds;
2 table spoons shelled pistachios

1 Dry roast or toast all ingredients for a few minutes (they'll start to pop), then grind in a mortar and pestle to crumbs. Serve in a separate bowl.

for a GFree version

For a GFree couscous use cauliflower 'rice' ~ break a cauli into florets, toss a teaspoon of turmeric into boiling salted water and add the cauli. Blanche for a minute, drain and blitz briefly in a food processor to turn into 'rice'.

Life in Fez

... is full of hustle and bustle and is a fascinating feast for the eyes

This menu is a tribute to our time there. The preserved lemon conjures up our magical memories - it's a must-have ingredient.

for the tagine

1 sweet potato, peeled, halved then cut into long wedge-shaped chunks

3 carrots, peeled & cut into thirds, then halved lengthways

1 table spoon sunflower oil

1 red onion, chopped

1 tea spoon ground ginger

1 tea spoon ground cumin

1 tea spoon paprika

1 tea spoon ground fennel

1 tea spoon ground cardamom

1 tea spoon turmeric or 'ras el hanout' blend

400g cooked chick peas

4 or 5 fresh medjool dates, stoned & cut into quarters

zest of 1 orange

1 preserved lemon, thinly sliced

large handful of fresh flat-leaved parsley, chopped

handful of fresh coriander, chopped

salt & pepper to season

1 Part-boil the sweet potato and carrot together in the same pan. Drain but keep the water for the couscous.

2 Heat the oil in a heavy based pan or tagine, add onion and stir. Add all the spices and 100ml of the reserved water and mix vigorously to a fine smooth paste (add a little more water if needed).

3 Fold the chickpeas into the spices. Layer over the sweet potato and carrots, plus the orange zest. Add the chopped dates and preserved lemon, piling them on top of each other rather than mixing in too much.

4 Cover with a heavy lid or the tagine lid and simmer very slowly for an hour. You can do this on top of the oven or in it. Just before serving add the parsley and coriander. Serve from the tagine or pan.

Flat Bread

makes 4 or 6

1 Sift dry ingredients (except seeds) into a large mixing bowl. Mix the milk and oil and drizzle into the flour mixture, folding sides to centre. Knead with a processor dough hook on a slow-speed setting for 5 minutes or knead by hand for 10 minutes until soft but pliable. Cover with a damp cloth and leave in a warm place for 20 minutes.

2 Turn on the grill and place a baking tray on the highest shelf 5 minutes before rolling out the dough. Lightly flatten the dough to a thick oblong on a floured surface and cut into 4 or 6. Roll out to flatten the dough, then sprinkle over the seeds and continue to roll, pressing the seeds in and rolling out to a thin irregular shape.

3 Place the breads on the HOT baking tray and pop back under the grill for just 1 or 2 minutes until browned.

Remove & serve immediately or keep warm in a tea towel until all the breads are grilled

for the flat bread

250g plain flour
1 tea spoon baking powder
1 tea spoon bicarbonate of soda
½ tea spoon salt
120ml of milk (soya or almond)
2 table spoons olive oil
nigella or sesame or lin seeds

Ginger

~ food of the gods

Aromatic, pungent and spicy, ginger adds a special flavour and zest to many fruit and vegetable dishes. Prized for it's aromatic, culinary and medicinal properties, the ancient Romans imported ginger from China 2000 years ago. It alleviates symptoms of gastrointestinal distress including motion & seasickness and contains very potent anti-inflammatory compounds called gingerols, the main active components and the ones responsible for its distinctive flavour. These therapeutic compounds include antioxidants, anti-tumour and anti-inflammatory effects.

Help yourself by generously adding ginger to your diet today

Fresh is best, but powdered, pickled, crystallised and candied ginger are great too ~ peel, slice, dice and use in both savoury and sweet dishes.

Gado-Gado

Gado-gado is one of the most well-known dishes from Indonesia. It literally means "mix mix" and is made of a rich mixture of vegetables generously served with a spiced peanut sauce dressing, and sometimes also topped with a hard boiled egg. Make it 'hot hot 'by adding more chilli if you dare

1 Place all the sauce ingredients in a food processor with 100ml of the water to start and blitz until well mixed. Drizzle in more water to make the sauce thinner as required ~ it should be neither too thick nor too runny.

2 Drain the tofu well by pressing dry between two sheets of kitchen paper. Cut into cubes and sauté in 2 table spoons of the sesame oil over a moderate heat until all sides are browned. Set aside.

3 Steam or blanche the broccoli, green beans and cabbage. Drain and keep warm wrapped in a tea towel.

4 Prepare all the other ingredients and mix with the vegetables in a large serving dish or ideally in individual bowls. Gently heat the sauce in a pan then remove from the heat as it starts to boil.

5 Pour over the vegetables, pile the sautéed tofu on top and garnish with the coriander and bean sprouts (and quartered eggs, if using).

Serve immediately with vermicelli noodles, egg noodles or steamed rice & flat breads. Can also be served cold on a hot summer's day for a light, refreshing meal. Thread the tofu cubes onto kebab sticks for a different final look if you fancy. Oh ~ and get those chop sticks going. Serves 4

for the sauce

150g salted peanuts
½ red onion, roughly chopped
4 garlic cloves, peeled
1 red hot chilli, roughly chopped
2 cms fresh ginger root, grated
3 table spoons good quality soy sauce
juice of 1 large lime
2 tea spoons brown sugar
100ml - 150ml water

for the Gado-Gado

1 packet firm tofu, drained & cubed
4 table spoons sesame oil
half a broccoli head, in florets
100g green beans, or mange tout
100g white cabbage, shredded
1 large carrot, grated
¼ cucumber, sliced into rounds
fresh bean sprouts to garnish

to garnish

1 handful fresh coriander
4 hard-boiled eggs, optional

29

Cardamom

Cardamom is an ancient exotic spice with exceptional health benefits and a very distinctive flavour suitable for both savoury and sweet dishes. The pods are preferred if possible, as they hold their flavour and health benefits better than when in the powdered form. It is high in antioxidants and has proven benefits against depression, asthma, bronchitis, colds and flu and is also renowned for its nourishing skin, complexion and hair properties.

beat the blues with this tasty bowl of benefits today

Buddha would have approved

... of such a bountiful bowl of awesomeness. Everything packs a punch in this nutritious, delicious, easy to make combination of colourful foods. Quinoa, sacred grain of the Incas, has exceptional nutritional qualities, as do lentils, chick peas, cumin, lemon and goji berries.

serves 6

^{200}g quinoa

^{1}tea spoon vegetable stock

^{100}g puy lentils, rinsed

^{400}g/1 jar chick peas, drained

^{1}table spoon olive oil

^{2}leeks, washed & sliced

^{1}red onion, chopped

^{1}red pepper, chopped

^{1}yellow pepper, chopped

^{2}green cardamom pods, split open

^{1}tea spoon cumin seeds

^{2}carrots, peeled & grated

^{2}table spoons soy sauce

^{1}table spoon balsamic vinegar

½ lemon, juiced

^{3}garlic cloves, crushed

^{35}g goji berries

handful fresh coriander

1 Cook the quinoa in a pan with twice the amount in volume of water and add the vegetable stock. Drain and set aside. Cook the puy lentils, unsalted, drain and set aside.

2 Heat the oil gently in a large pan (with lid), adding the leeks, onion and peppers, stirring frequently for 5 minutes.

3 Spilt open the cardamom pods, grind the seeds together with the cumin seeds and add to the leeks. Stir in the carrots, place the lid on top and simmer gently for a further 5 minutes. Turn off the heat and leave in the pan till ready to serve.

4 Whilst the quinoa & lentils are still warm, mix together with the chick peas, soy sauce, balsamic vinegar, lemon juice, garlic and goji berries. Gently stir together to incorporate and leave for 5 minutes.

5 Scoop into individual bowls, pile a serving of the leek mixture on top and add a final scattering of coriander.

Our home grown Shiitake mushrooms

We've grown shiitake mushrooms in our woodlands using an ancient Japanese method. Holes are drilled into freshly cut oak logs, inoculated with a live culture of shiitake mycelium, then sealed with wax and left in a damp and dappled part of the woods to allow the mycelium to colonise the log. Up to 3 times a year, the logs are left overnight in our river to mimic a natural downpour and induce the mycelium to fruit. A log can continue to produce for up to 5 years.

Just look at Seany showing off a recent flush

The medicinal magic of this mushroom

Low in fat and calories but high in nutritional content, the shiitake is a rich source of the B vitamins ~ B1 (thiamine), B2 (riboflavin), B3 (niacin), B5 (pantothenic acid), B6 and B9 (folate), as well as vitamins C and D. It's high in the minerals magnesium, manganese, iron, phosphorus, zinc, selenium and potassium.

Gosh. Who knew?

To maximize their nutty flavour and retain nutrients, don't overcook ~ a quick sauté for 7 minutes does the trick. Clean with a brush or damp paper towel, then store in a loose paper bag in the fridge to maintain their health benefits.

Shiitake Mushroom Stir Fry
with cashews & smoked tofu

A so-good-for-you stir fry that takes minutes to make. Most mushrooms are pretty marvellous when it comes to their health benefits, but the shiitake is the samurai of them all, considered medicinal in the many Asian countries where it originates from

1 Have all your ingredients ready to make the most of the quickness of a stir fry. Heat a wok or frying pan with 2 table spoons of the sesame oil on a low to moderate heat.

2 Throw in the shiitakes and sauté for seven minutes, stirring constantly. Remove to a plate.

3 Add the remaining 2 table spoons of oil and stir fry the tofu & red onion until they're browned. Remove to the shiitake plate.

4 Mix the Chinese spice with the cornflour, tamari and water to a fine paste then add the ginger and garlic. Pour into the wok, stirring constantly for a minute as it thickens, adding the cashews.

5 Turn off the heat, toss in the shiitakes, tofu and onion. Mix well, squeeze over the lemon juice and coriander.

Serve immediately with your choice of veg & noodles

250g shiitake mushrooms, brushed clean, sliced thickly, hard stalks discarded

4 table spoons sesame oil

1 red onion, chopped

200g smoked tofu, patted dry, sliced into matchsticks

1 thumb-size piece fresh ginger, peeled & grated

3 cloves smoked garlic, crushed

1 tea spoon Chinese '5 spice' mix

1 dessert spoon cornflour

50ml tamari sauce, plus 100ml water

50g cashew nuts

bunch of coriander

½ lemon, juiced

Want to go GFree?

easily done

Forget the filo wrap and simply put in a baking dish
sprinkling sesame seeds over the top. Delicious as
pie, without wheat, barley or rye.

Feta & Red Pepper Filo Wrap
with leek & spinach

Light and fluffy, this easy pie is great as a side dish or filling enough to be the main star of the show

1 Pre-heat the oven to 190C / gas 5. Grease and line a deep rectangle or oval baking dish.

2 Bring a pan of water to the boil, add the vegetable stock and leeks and blanche for 2 minutes. Drain the leeks in a colander. Wash the spinach leaves and pat dry, then mix with the leeks. Separate the eggs.

3 In a large bowl, mash the feta with a fork and mix in the yoghurt and oregano. Crush in the garlic and add the egg yolks. Toss in the leek and spinach mixture. Stir through.

4 Add a pinch of salt to the egg whites and whisk to stiff white peaks (about 2 minutes). Gently fold into the feta mixture in batches.

5 Brush each filo sheet with the olive oil and place all 5 sheets in the lined baking dish, leaving enough pastry over one edge to wrap over as a cover. Pour in half the feta mix. Arrange the slices of red pepper over, then pour in the remaining feta mix. Wrap the excess filo over the top and tuck in the edges.

6 Gently score the top and brush with the remaining oil. Bake for about 30 to 40 minutes until golden brown on top.

Allow to rest a few minutes before serving with oven roasted seasonal veg or a variety of slaws and salads. Have a slice of pie cold for a lovely 'left-over' treat the next day

serves 4 - 6

1 leek, outer leaves discarded, sliced into rounds & washed

1 cube vegetable stock

100g spinach leaves, dry weight, stalks removed

1 packet feta cheese (200g)

1 tub natural greek yoghurt (125g)

1 tea spoon dried oregano

2 garlic cloves

3 eggs, separated

4 slices roasted red pepper

2 table spoons olive oil

5 sheets ready-rolled filo pastry

Oranges are a vitamin goldmine

They help the heart, tonify the skin, boost the immune system, can lower blood sugar levels, can lower the risk of cataracts, and can protect against obesity.

Cooking them into a cake is a cracking way to make the most of these mighty marvels.

Did you know

Wonderfully delicious pistachio nuts have been revered as the symbol of wellness and robust health since ancient times

It takes 8 to 10 years from plantation to bear fruit. Wow! After that first crop though it keeps bearing fruit for many years to come. Similarly, it takes an age to get the kernel out of it's protective outer shell, but once done, it's well worth the effort. Pistachios are an excellent source of vitamin E, carotenes, antioxidants, proteins and important minerals, particularly copper and iron. They can lower bad LDL cholesterol and increase good HDL cholesterol reducing the overall risk of heart disease and strokes.

Pack Pistachios into your diet today.

Orange Pistachio Pudding Cake

2 large oranges, washed & quartered

(prepped an hour ahead of the rest of the cake)

4 free range organic eggs

190g castor sugar

200g ground almond powder

50g maïs or corn flour

1 tea spoon baking powder

1 tea spoon bicarbonate of soda

2 tea spoons ginger

1 tea spoon cinnamon

50ml olive oil

2 table spoons maple syrup

100g pistachios, shelled & smashed

It's great as it is, or you might want to spread some marmalade mixed with maple syrup over the top.

Or spread with a spoonful of apricot jam and sprinkle over some grated coconut.

Or top with a dollop of crème fraîche.

1 Wash the skin of the oranges, quarter and bring to the boil in a pan of water. Once boiled, simmer for an hour at least. Drain very well and cool, picking out any pips.

2 Heat the oven to 190C / gas 5 and line a rectangle baking tin or round spring-form cake tin.

3 Put the cooled oranges, including skin and pith, into a food processor and blitz to a coarse pulp. Add the eggs, sugar and blitz again for 5 seconds. Then add all other ingredients except the pistachios and blitz for 30 seconds.

3 Stir in 90g of the pistachios.

4 Pour into the baking tin then sprinkle over the remaining pistachios and bake for an hour, or until a skewer inserted in the middle comes out clean.

Walnut Biscotti

1 Heat the oven to 180C/ gas 4.

2 Sift together the flour, baking powder, bicarbonate of soda and cinnamon into a large bowl. Separately, beat the sugar and eggs until pale & fluffy, add the salt and orange zest. Make a well in the centre of the flour mixture and gradually pour in the creamed sugar & eggs. Mix very well together, add the walnuts and mix again to a sticky dough.

3 It's quite tricky to handle, so flour your hands, turn out onto floured baking paper and form into a long rectangle, rounded at the ends. Lift the baking paper gently onto a baking tray and bake for 20 to 25 minutes, until golden brown. The mixture will spread and rise as it cooks.

4 Remove from the oven, allow to cool for 10 minutes, then cut into slices still on the baking tray. Turn off the oven and pop the tray back in for 15 minutes for the biscotti to set.

Gorgeous with a warmed bowl of soup, with a selection of cheeses to pile on top or have your biscotti just as they are with a lovely cup of tea or coffee

200g plain flour

1 tea spoon baking powder

1 tea spoon bicarbonate of soda

1 tea spoon cinnamon

200g castor sugar

2 eggs

½ tea spoon salt

zest of 1 orange

100g walnuts crushed

Go nuts with wonderful walnuts. Nature has crafted a near perfect package of protein, healthy fats, fibre, antioxidants and many vitamins and minerals in the walnut. Rich in omega-3 fats and containing higher amounts of antioxidants than most other foods, eating walnuts may improve brain health while also helping to prevent heart disease and cancer.

our walnut tree Wilma

Date & Walnut Slice

Be transported to the shores of the Nile with a delightful slice of date & walnut cake to snack on. Dating back 6,000 years to ancient Egypt & Mesopotamia, the durable date is distinguished among foods as an excellent source of essential vitamins, minerals and much needed dietary fibre

1 Heat the oven to 190C / gas 5. Grease and line a loaf tin.

2 Put the chopped dates into a large bowl, add the bicarbonate of soda, margarine or butter and cover with the boiling water. Let cool for 5 minutes.

3 Sift the flour and baking powder into the date mix and add all other ingredients.

4 Mix well then pour into the loaf tin and bake for an hour. Check the top isn't burning, cover if necessary and continue cooking until a knife comes out clean. Let rest before turning out onto a rack to cool.

Snaz up a slice by adding some hot maple syrup drizzled over a scoop of cold caramel ice-cream & scatter with toasted walnuts ~ definitely delicious

And when it comes to cakes, walnuts and dates are best mates to bake. Chewy, sticky, nutty and very more-ish. Although super to snack on and despite their impressive nutrient-rich credentials essential to good health, dates are a sugar bomb so don't be tempted to over-do digesting them.

250g dates, chopped

1 tea spoon bicarbonate of soda

15g margarine or butter

250ml boiling water

65ml sunflower oil

250g flour

1 tea spoon baking powder

180g brown sugar

1 table spoon maple syrup

100g walnuts, crushed

Spiced Summer Fruit Tarts

Making the most of all the fabulous fresh fruits in our garden is a must. Once harvested, the next important thing to do is use them up. Jams & chutneys are an option of course, but oh, all that sugar. So here's a simple way to put a smile on faces with a refreshingly spiced summer fruit tart full of natural flavour and naturally good for you

the basics
~ quick almond paste

80g margarine or butter

100g almond flour

1 tea spoon ginger

1 tea spoon cinnamon

2 table spoons maple syrup

1 tea spoon almond extract

dash of water if needed

1 packet ready rolled flaky pastry, or make your own of course

Classic Apple Tart

4 or 5 apples (they don't have to be cooking apples) washed, cored & sliced

1 lemon, juiced

1 table spoon cognac/brandy

handful of grated coconut to garnish

1 Heat the oven to 190C / gas 5.

2 Place the sliced apples in a bowl and stir in the lemon juice and cognac.

3 For the almond paste: Melt the margarine or butter in a pan, adding all the other ingredients except the water, stirring frequently. It's a thick consistency but needs to be spreadable, so add a dash of water if needed. Take off the heat and cool slightly.

4 Roll out your pastry into a greased tart tin. Use a metal spoon to scoop dollops of the almond paste into the pastry case spreading to the edges with the back of the spoon.

5 Place the apple slices onto the paste and bake for 35 minutes until the pastry is browned. Sprinkle over the coconut when ready to serve.

Apricot Tart with Walnuts

250g apricots, halved & stoned

1 table spoon cognac/brandy

50g walnuts, broken

1 Prepare the apricots by slitting them horizontally to get the stone out. Place all the cut halves in a bowl and stir in the cognac.

2 Prepare the almond paste as for the Classic Apple recipe.

3 Place the apricot halves, cut side down, onto the paste and pack them all in tightly. Scatter over the walnuts and bake for 35 minutes until the pastry is browned.

Fig Tart

250g figs

1 table spoon cognac/brandy

1 Prepare the figs by cutting some in half and some into quarters and placing them all in a bowl with the cognac.

2 Prepare the almond paste as for the Classic Apple recipe.

3 Place the figs onto the paste and pack them all in tightly. Bake for 35 minutes until the pastry is browned.

Go GFree with Chestnuts

Wow your guests with this guilt-free delight

A luxuriously filling and impressive dessert to wow your guests with! Its packed with good-for-you ingredients so doesn't come with the usual guilt-trip associated with rich desserts. It's also very easy to make and keeps in the freezer - if there's any to spare, that is. Can be made the same day, allowing 2 to 3 hours of chilling time or the night before and chilled overnight.

It's great on it's own

... or topped with a frozen fruit blush of raspberry, strawberry or mango sorbets (or a mixture of all 3) and a scattering of fresh seasonal berries

... or drizzled with cream and a hint of mint.

Chestnuts lend themselves to all things sweet as well as savoury. They are naturally high in starch meaning they are a good source of energy without the calories or fat to match. They are nutritionally high in dietary fibre, folates, and minerals and exceptionally high in vitamin C. True to the nature of nuts, they are an excellent source of B vitamins and like almonds and hazelnuts, free from gluten making them an important and versatile food source for those who need to have a GFree diet.

Rich Dark Chocolate & Chestnut Cheesecake

1 Grease and line a 24cm round or a 20 x 25cm rectangle cake tin.

2 Break up the ginger nuts in a food processor until they start to crumble. Melt the margarine or butter then pour over the ginger nuts and continue to process until fine breadcrumbs. The mixture should begin to fall off the sides of the processor. Press down and evenly into the tin and chill in the freezer until the filling is ready.

3 Put the chestnuts in a food processor with the sugar and process until fairly smooth. Keep in the processor. Break up the chocolate and put in a pan with the coconut cream. Heat and stir gently until they are melted together to a smooth sauce. Stir in the vanilla extract, cognac if using and orange zest. Take off the heat and cool for a minute before pouring over the chestnut mix. Blend until smooth but still softly textured.

4 Remove the base from the freezer and pour in the chocolate mix. Gently spread evenly over the surface. Freeze over-night or for 2 or 3 hours if making on the same day. In either case, take out and leave in the fridge for an hour before serving.

Serve chilled. Serves 12

for the base

1 packet ginger nut biscuits (250g)

75g margarine or butter

for the filling

400g cooked chestnuts, vacuum packed or jarred

80g caster sugar

100g dark chocolate with orange pieces

5 tbs coconut cream

1 tsp vanilla extract

2 tbs cognac (optional)

zest of 1 orange

Decadent and delightful

for the veggie version

Use butter instead of margarine and replace all the tofu list of ingredients with 3 free range, organic eggs. Whisk these with the sugar until pale and fluffy then add to the rest of the filling mix. Bake at the same temperature for the same length of time.

Using six plump lemons in the filling, this is a rich, moist, decadent lemony dessert to end any delightful dinner. It's the perfect melt-in-the-mouth combination of soft tangy lemon contrasted with short crumbly pastry. Here's two versions to taste … veggie & vegan.

Switch the ground almonds for ground hazelnuts if preferred, though it changes little in the final finish. What will make a difference is whether the almonds or hazelnuts are whitened or not. Unbleached powdered nuts will come out darker in colour.

for a GFree version

Simply replace the plain flour with 100g rice flour mixed with 50g maïs or corn flour.

for the pastry

150g plain flour

50g ground almonds

150g cold margarine, diced

50g castor sugar

1 tea spoon bicarbonate of soda

1 table spoon cold water

for the filling

6 plump lemons

200g castor sugar

150g margarine, melted

100g ground almonds

30g grated coconut

for the vegan version

300g tofu

1 tea spoon Dijon mustard

½ tea spoon salt

1 table spoon sugar

2 table spoons apple cider vinegar

Pop in the fridge until ready to serve, which might be immediately, having worked up such an appetite. Add a scoop of something gooey, drizzle with a dash of maple syrup and sprinkle with grated coconut.

Tarte au Citron

1 Heat the oven to 180C / gas 4 and line a tart or flan dish.

2 For the pastry: Put the flour, ground almonds and margarine in a processor and whizz until fine breadcrumbs. Add the sugar, bicarbonate of soda and whizz again, whilst drizzling in the water. Whizz until the mixture starts to come together, adding a dash more water if needed. Form into a ball with your hands, wrap in clingfilm and refrigerate for up to an hour.

3 Then roll out the pastry thinly onto lightly floured baking paper. Lift the paper and place into the tart dish. Line with more baking paper, covering the edges, and fill with baking beans. Bake blind for 10 minutes, remove from the oven to cool slightly before removing the baking paper and beans. Pop the case back in the oven for 2 or 3 minutes, remove again and cool completely.

4 For the filling: Melt the margarine gently and zest in 3 of the lemons. Turn off the heat, add the ground almonds, coconut and the juice of all 6 lemons. Blitz all the tofu ingredients together and stir in the castor sugar before adding to the filling mix.

5 Pour into the pastry case and bake for about 30 minutes, until gently golden. Leave to cool.

Banana Coconut Ice Cream

Bananas have made it 'to print' once again. Featured in my first book, they're a big part of life here at UTLT. Our plant is still going strong and still takes centre stage in the courtyard. The wow factor at the end of dinner defies the simplicity of this recipe ~ always store bananas in your freezer and you'll never be short of something sensational to finish with

1 Take the peeled bananas out of the freezer 5 minutes before you are ready to work with them.

2 Chop roughly into a food processor and add all of the coconut cream. Whizz until smooth.

3 Toast the pine nuts. Scoop the banana coconut cream into 4 separate glasses and top immediately with a sprinkle of ginger, the pine nuts and blueberries.

Et voilà ~ that's all folks!

serves 4

4 bananas, peeled from the freezer
200ml carton of coconut cream, chilled
1 tea spoon powdered ginger
handful of pine nuts, toasted
blueberries to garnish

A Traditional Shortbread recipe
~ from a traditional Scottish person

The wee mammy of my dear Scottish friend, Flaherty, has spent a lifetime making this delicious shortbread-to-die for. So here it is, Mary Laurie Fairbairn's shortbread

1 Heat oven to 160C / gas 4. Keep your hands and working surface nice and cool during preparation.

2 Knead the butter into the sugar with a little of the flour. Add the rest of the flour gradually. Turn out onto a piece of floured baking paper and roll into shape - round or rectangle - maintaining a 1 cm thickness, so don't over roll it. Jab through with a fork.

3 Bake for approximately 30 to 40 minutes until beginning to turn a lovely golden colour. Cool on a rack but slice while still warm and sprinkle with a little castor sugar.

Being me, I've used a mixture of rice & maïs flours to make it GFree. I've added a tea spoon of powdered ginger to make it softly spicy; I've added crystallised ginger pieces; dried apricot pieces & generally experimented with an age old recipe. Make it your own, by adding a little of what you like

100g plain flour
50g butter, cold & diced
25g sugar

Using the same ratio of flour, butter & sugar, you can easily double or triple the quantity to make even more yummy shortbread-to-die for

47

Lightning Source UK Ltd.
Milton Keynes UK
UKRC02n2231140317
296641UK00005B/19

* 9 7 8 1 9 0 8 0 0 0 3 4 7 *